D0404274

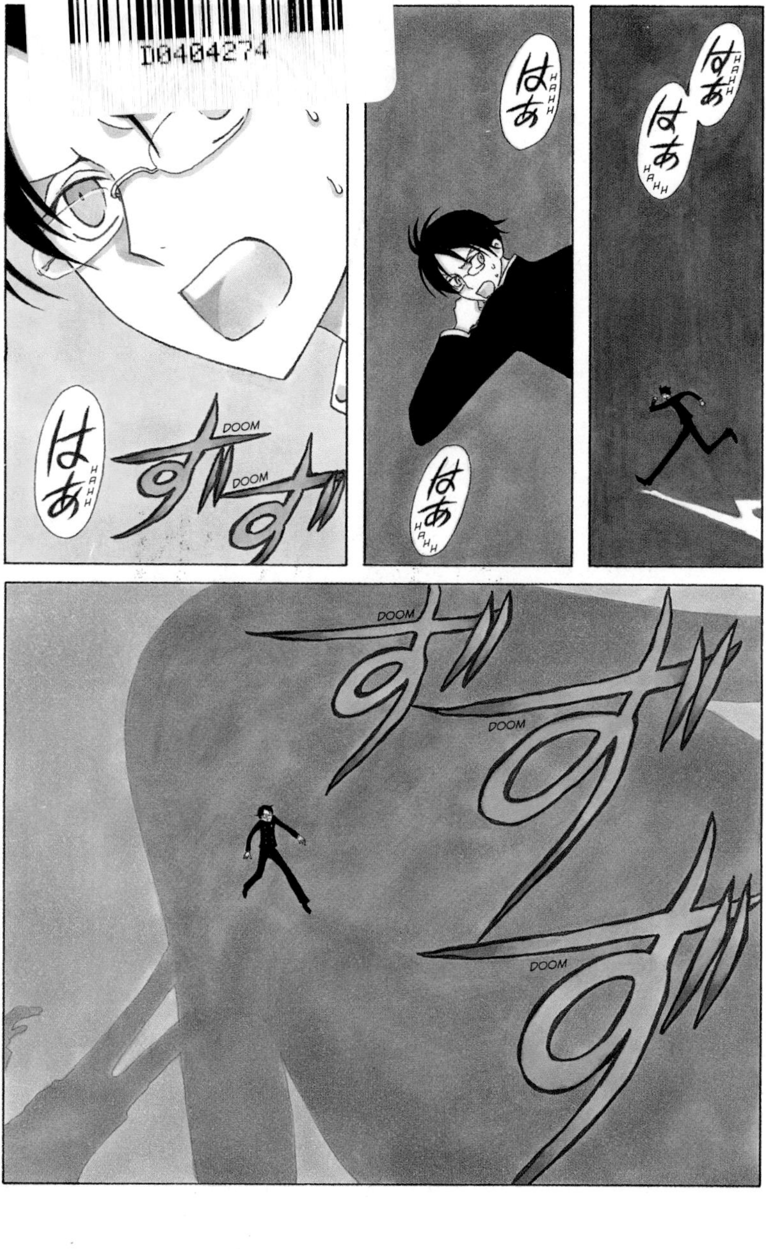

ずずず
DOOM
DOOM
DOOM

xxxHOLiC
〜×××ホリック〜

GYAAAAAH!!!

9

CLAMP

TRANSLATED AND ADAPTED BY

William Flanagan

LETTERED BY

Dana Hayward

BALLANTINE BOOKS • NEW YORK

xxxHOLiC, volume 9 is a work of fiction. Names, characters, places, and incidents are the products of the author's imagination or are used fictitiously. Any resemblance to actual events, locales, or persons, living or dead, is entirely coincidental.

A Del Rey Trade Paperback Original

xxxHOLiC Vol. 9 copyright © 2006 by CLAMP

English translation copyright © 2006 by CLAMP

All rights reserved.

Published in the United States by Del Rey Books, an imprint of The Random House Publishing Group, a division of Random House, Inc., New York.

Del Rey is a registered trademark and the Del Rey colophon is a trademark of Random House, Inc.

Publication rights arranged through Kodansha Ltd.

First published in Japan in 2006 by Kodansha Ltd., Tokyo.

ISBN 978-0-345-49639-3

Printed in the United States of America

www.delreymanga.com

9 8 7 6 5 4 3 2 1

Translator and Adaptor—William Flanagan
Lettering—Dana Hayward

xxxHOLiC crosses over with *Tsubasa*. Although it isn't necessary to read *Tsubasa* to understand the events in *xxxHOLiC*, you'll get to see the same events from different perspectives if you read both series!

Contents

Honorifics Explained

Throughout the Del Rey Manga books, you will find Japanese honorifics left intact in the translations. For those not familiar with how the Japanese use honorifics and, more important, how they differ from American honorifics, we present this brief overview.

Politeness has always been a critical facet of Japanese culture. Ever since the feudal era, when Japan was a highly stratified society, use of honorifics—which can be defined as polite speech that indicates relationship or status—has played an essential role in the Japanese language. When addressing someone in Japanese, an honorific usually takes the form of a suffix attached to one's name (example: "Asuna-san"), or as a title at the end of one's name or in place of the name itself (example: "Negi-sensei," or simply "Sensei!").

Honorifics can be expressions of respect or endearment. In the context of manga and anime, honorifics give insight into the nature of the relationship between characters. Many English translations leave out these important honorifics, and therefore distort the feel of the original Japanese. Because Japanese honorifics contain nuances that English honorifics lack, it is our policy at Del Rey not to translate them. Here, instead, is a guide to some of the honorifics you may encounter in Del Rey Manga.

-san: This is the most common honorific, and is equivalent to Mr., Miss, Ms., Mrs. It is the all-purpose honorific and can be used in any situation where politeness is required.

-sama: This is one level higher than "-san" and it is used to confer great respect.

-dono: This comes from the word "tono," which means "lord." It is an even higher level than "-sama" and confers utmost respect.

-kun: This suffix is used at the end of boys' names to express familiarity or endearment. It is also sometimes used by men amongst friends, or when addressing someone younger or of a lower station.

-chan: This is used to express endearment, mostly toward girls. It is also used for little boys, pets, and even among lovers. It gives a sense of childish cuteness.

Bozu: This is an informal way to refer to a boy, similar to the English term "kid" or "squirt."

Sempai/Senpai: This title suggests that the addressee is one's senior in a group or organization. It is most often used in a school setting, where underclassmen refer to their upperclassmen as "sempai." It can also be used in the workplace, such as when a newer employee addresses an employee who has seniority in the company.

Kohai: This is the opposite of "sempai," and is used toward underclassmen in school or newcomers in the workplace. It connotes that the addressee is of a lower station.

Sensei: Literally meaning "one who has come before," this title is used for teachers, doctors, or masters of any profession or art.

-[blank]: This is usually forgotten in these lists, but it is perhaps the most significant difference between Japanese and English. The lack of honorific means that the speaker has permission to address the person in a very intimate way. Usually, only family, spouses, or very close friends have this kind of permission. Known as *yobisute*, it can be gratifying when someone who has earned the intimacy starts to call one by one's name without an honorific. But when that intimacy hasn't been earned, it can be very insulting.

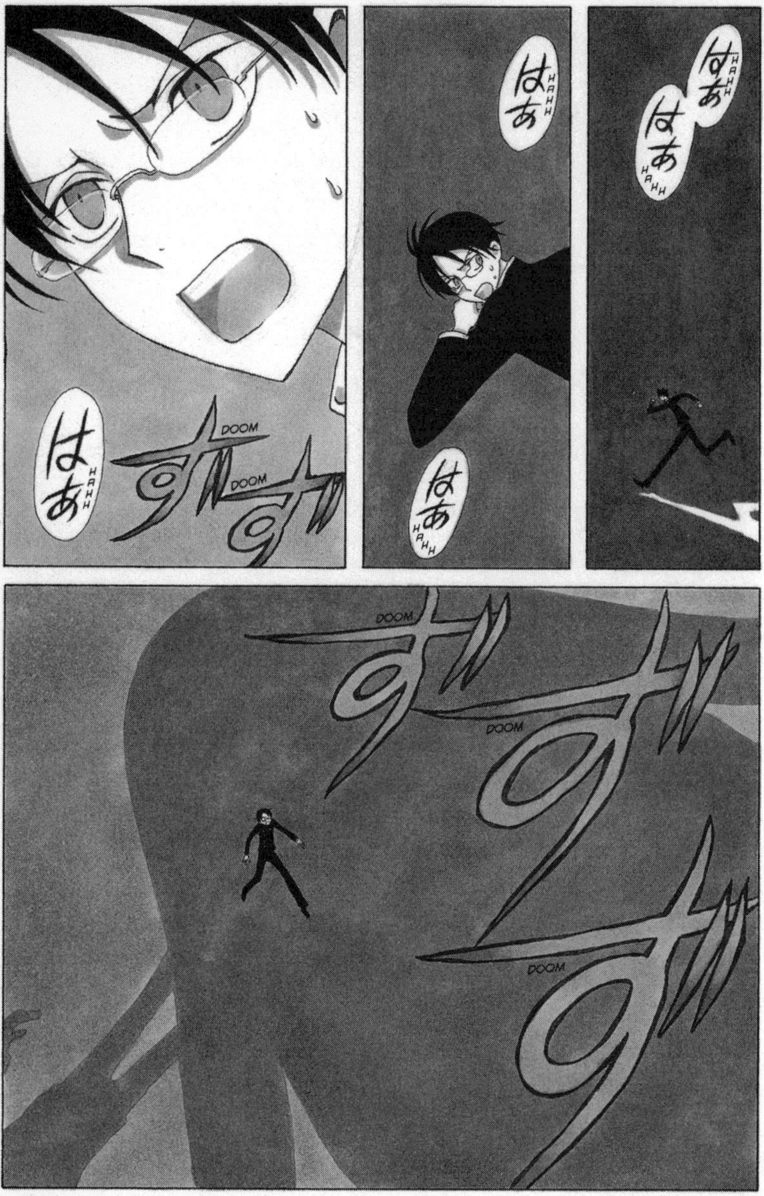

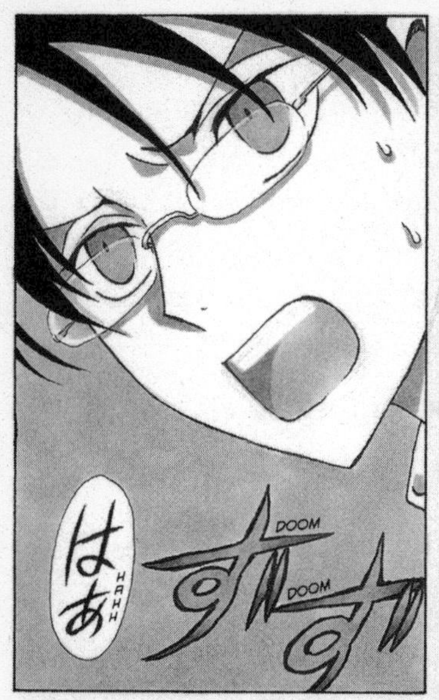

DOOM
DOOM
DOOM

xxxHOLiC
×××ホリック

GYAAAAAH!!!

......
AND SO...
THAT WAS THE FIRST DREAM OF THE YEAR FOR ME.

WHAT A CUTE DREAM!
Y-YOU THINK IT'S CUTE...?

I THINK IT'S AMAZINGLY CUTE!!
SMILE
SLUMP

HIMAWARI-CHAN REALLY IS INCREDIBLE! AND HER SMILE IS JUST DIVINE!
PAAAA
BESIDES, IT HAS AN EGGPLANT IN IT, SO IT *MUST* BE A GOOD DREAM!

DON'T THEY SAY THAT #1 IS MOUNT FUJI, #2 IS A HAWK, AND #3 IS AN EGGPLANT?

I KNOW THAT MOUNT FUJI AND HAWKS HAVE A CERTAIN SENSE OF SOMETHING GOOD HAPPENING...
...BUT WHY AN EGG-PLANT, DO YOU SUPPOSE?
I WONDER.

WHAT WAS YOUR FIRST DREAM, HIMAWARI-CHAN?

IT WAS SORT OF A FRIGHTENING DREAM...

WH-WHAT WAS IT ABOUT?

UP TO THE MID-POINT, IT WAS MUCH LIKE YOURS…

I WAS WALKING THROUGH THE BLACKNESS, AND I HEARD FOOTSTEPS BEHIND ME…

AS I INCREASED MY PACE, THE SOUND OF THE FOOTSTEPS QUICKENED AS WELL.

I THOUGHT I'D SHAKE THE PURSUER OFF, SO I RAN AS FAST AS I COULD, BUT IT WAS NO USE.

AND LITTLE BY LITTLE THE THING GOT CLOSER.

SUDDENLY I REALIZED… IT FELT LIKE IT WAS RIGHT BEHIND ME.

I THOUGHT IT HAD CAUGHT UP…
…AND WHEN I TURNED TO LOOK…

OH!
THERE'S A CLASS REPRESENTATIVE MEETING THAT I HAVE TO ATTEND!
WHUMP

I KNOW IT'S IN THE MIDDLE OF MY STORY. SORRY!
NO... IT'S OKAY.
I JUST HIT MY HEAD A LITTLE.

WOW! THANK YOU!!
I'M ALWAYS GETTING THINGS FROM YOU! SORRY!
SHAKE
SHAKE
DON'T APOLOGIZE! I MADE THEM BECAUSE I WANTED TO.

OH, YEAH! HERE!
HERE ARE SOME MADELEINES I MADE YESTERDAY.

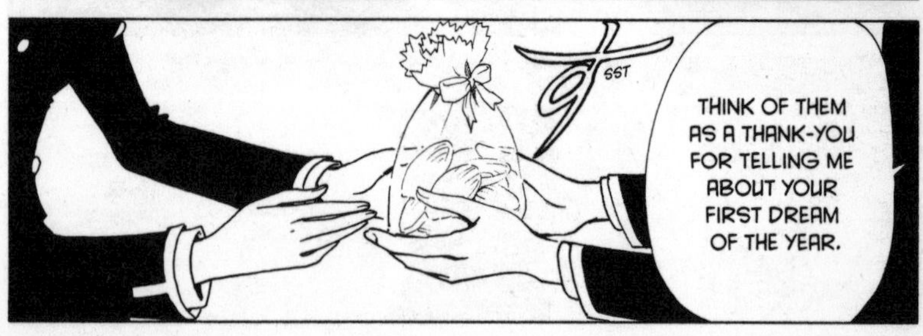
SST
THINK OF THEM AS A THANK-YOU FOR TELLING ME ABOUT YOUR FIRST DREAM OF THE YEAR.

......
EH?

I'LL SEE YOU SOON!
I LOOK FORWARD TO IT!

AH! I'LL MAKE SURE THAT DÔMEKI GETS SOME—

YOU DON'T HAVE TO DO THAT, REALLY!!
FWISH

THE EXPLANATION IS THAT IN THE OLDEN DAYS THE FIRST OF THE YEAR WAS WHEN THE VERY FIRST EGGPLANTS OF THE SEASON WERE HARVESTED, SO THEY WERE EXPENSIVE AND HARD TO OBTAIN.

THAT MAKES SENSE.

BUT!

I DON'T UNDERSTAND WHY I HAVE TO HELP YOU!!

VSSH

VSSH

BECAUSE YOU SAID YOU'D HELP IN KUNOGI'S PLACE.

FOLD

FOLD

BUT HIMAWARI-CHAN SAID...

...THAT A RELATIVE WAS VISITING HER HOME, SO SHE HAD TO BE THERE!

BUT THERE WERE LEAFLETS FROM THE REPRESENTA-TIVES' MEETING THAT SHE HAD TO WORK ON, AND SHE DIDN'T KNOW WHAT TO DO!

SO I HAD TO SAY, "I'LL GO HELP OUT! ♥" THAT'S ONLY NATURAL! AS A FELLOW HUMAN!

BUT!!

VSSH
I NEVER THOUGHT THAT I'D BE DOING IT WITH YOU!!
THE MORE YOU KEEP PLAYING, THE LATER YOU'LL GO HOME.

FOLD
おり
おり
FOLD
I'M NOT PLAYING!
I'M WORKING AS HARD AS I CAN!

BUT IF I HADN'T SWITCHED, THEN HIMAWARI-CHAN WOULD HAVE BEEN ALONE WITH DÔMEKI!
THINKING OF IT THAT WAY, THIS WAS A VERY GOOD DECISION.

LISTEN, YOU...
OH, SHUT UP!
CAN'T YOU FOLD THAT BETTER! CLUMSY DOLT!

THAT'S RIGHT! TWO PEOPLE ALONE AFTER SCHOOL IN THE CLASS REPRESENTATIVES' ROOM SEEMS KIND OF CLICHÉ.
IF SOME-THING HAD HAPPENED...
NO... HIMAWARI-CHAN WOULD NEVER... NOT WITH HIM! NOT A CHANCE. NOT EVER. NEVER, BUT...
ぱく
POK

THAT...!
IT CAN'T BE...!
IT'S...

むぐむぐ
MUNCH MUNCH

AREN'T THOSE THE THINGS THAT I MADE...?
YOU CAN'T TELL THE STUFF THAT YOU MADE YOURSELF?

THERE ARE TIMES WHEN A GUY KNOWS, BUT HE STILL WANTS TO MAKE SURE!!
GWAAH!
WHY ARE *YOU* EATING THEM?!

KUNOGI GAVE THEM TO ME.

I TOLD HER THAT SHE DIDN'T HAVE TO SHARE THEM WITH HIM!

AAAAAAH! HIMAWARI-CHAN!

TP
TP
?

GEEZ! DÔMEKI, THAT CREEP!
HE HAD ME MAKING COFFEE FOR HIM!
STOMP
STOMP

こつ
TAK
ぺた
TP
THE SOUND OF FOOT-STEPS?
こつ
TAK
ぺた
TP
こつ
TAK
ぺた
TP
こつ
TAK
ぺた
TP

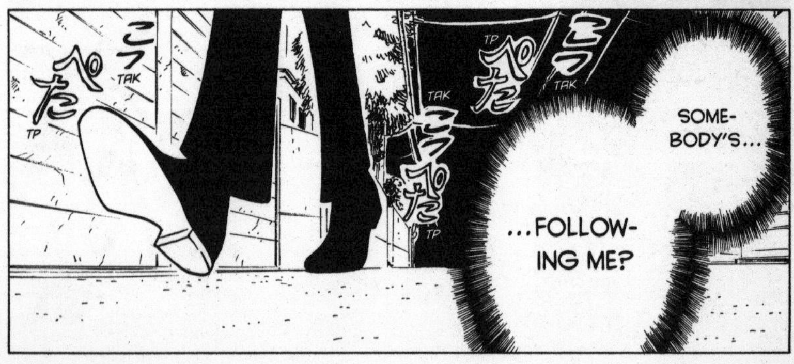

ぺた
TP
ぺた
TP

OH, HELL...
ぺた
TP

たっ
TMP
たっ
TMP

ぺた
TP
ぺた
TP

たっ
TMP
たっ
TMP
たっ
TMP

ぺた
TP
ぺた
TP
ぺた
TP

たっ TMP ぺた TP
たっ TMP ぺた TP
THAT'S...
たっ TMP ぺた TP
たっ TMP ぺた TP
たっ TMP ぺた TP
たっ TMP ぺた TP

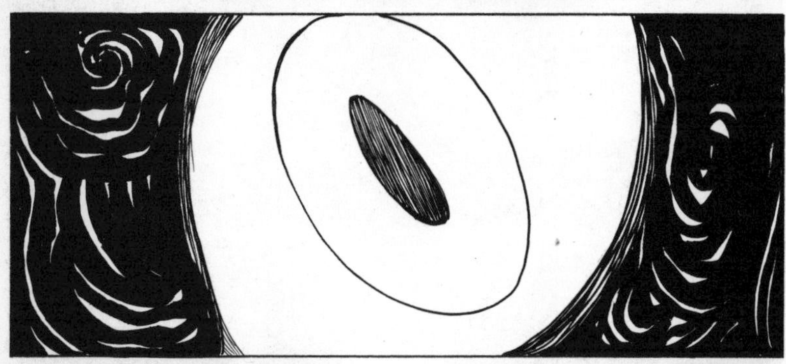

THIS
IS
BAD!

IT'S HUGE!

AND IT'S DANGEROUS!

IF IT CATCHES ME...!!

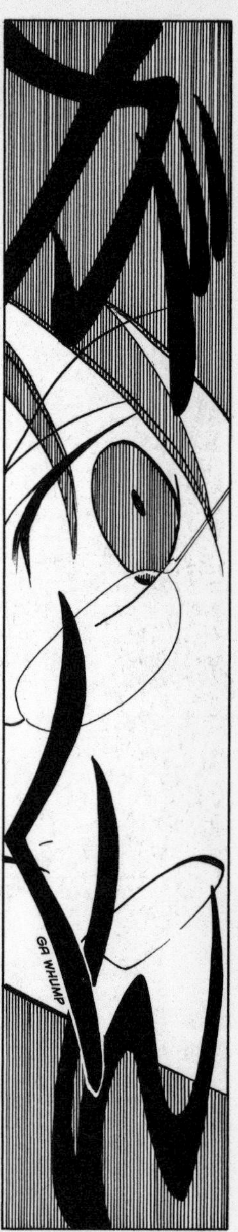

IT'S GOING TO EAT ME!!

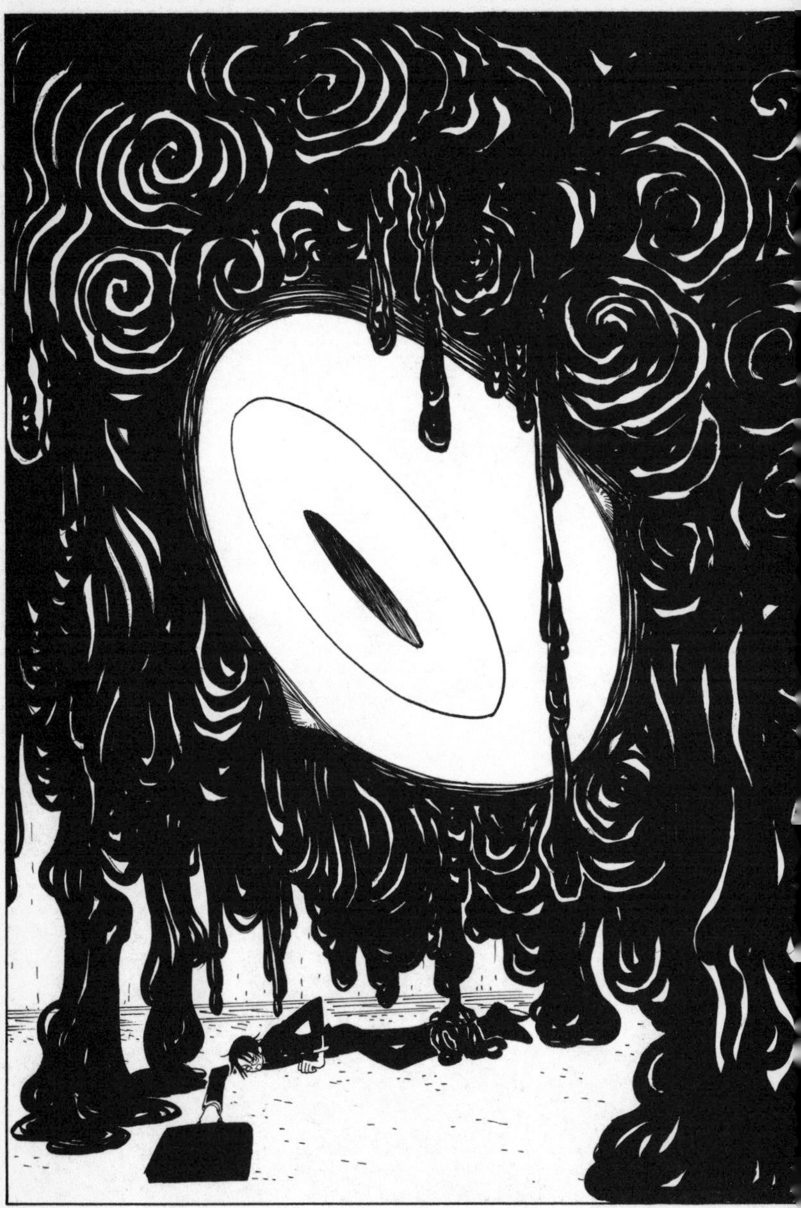

ずい
ZLM
ずい
ZLM

ずい
ZLM
ずい
ZLM

KLOP

STRCH

VWANG

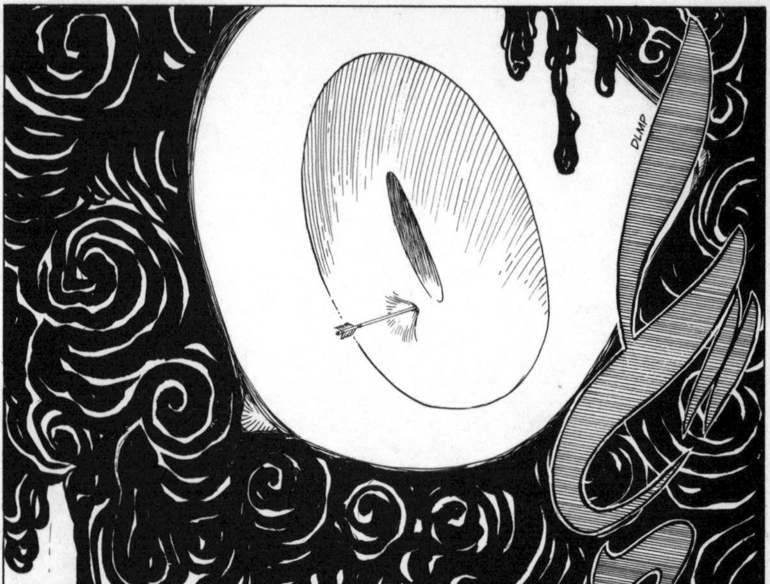

DLMP

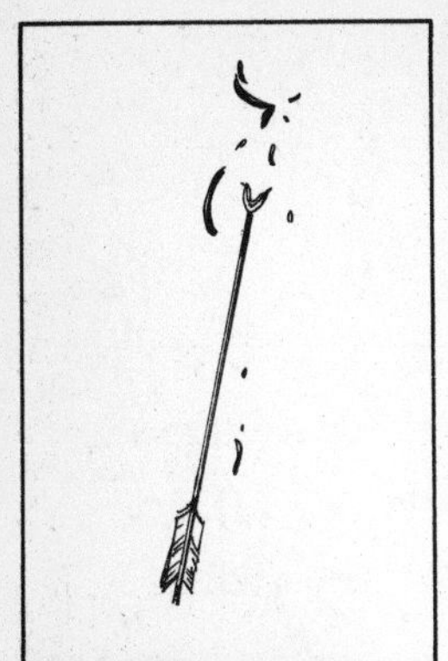

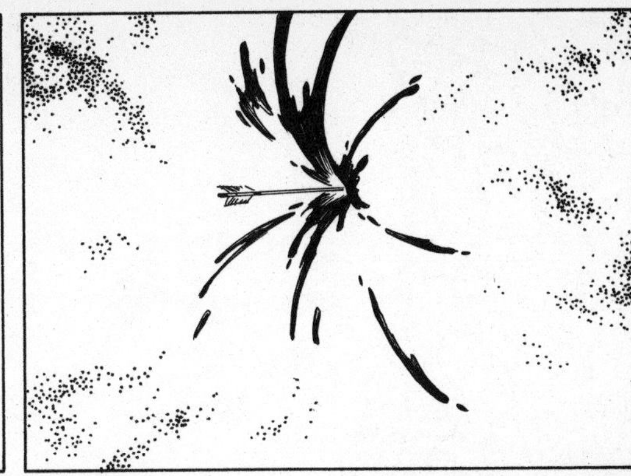

からん
KALANK

.....
DÔMEKI...

xxxHOLiC
〜×××ホリック〜

WHUMP

UNG!

HEY, IF YOU'RE GOING TO SLEEP IN THE MIDDLE OF THE ROAD, I'M GOING TO SIT ON YOU.

THAT WAS A DREAM.

YOU'RE SAYING...
...THAT THE HUGE THING THAT WAS GOING TO EAT ME AND DÔMEKI AND EVERYTHING...
WAS A DREAM?
SST
BUT...
...IF THAT'S TRUE, HOW CAN SOME-THING THAT'S JUST A DREAM MAKE ME FALL...
YOU HAVE IT WRONG.

IT'S A TRUE DREAM.
AH...?

A TRUE DREAM IS...
KREE
KREE
A DREAM THAT HAS SOMEHOW BECOME REAL, RIGHT?

KREE
THAT'S RIGHT.
OR TO BE MORE SPECIFIC, IT'S A DREAM THAT WILL LATER BECOME REALITY.

BUT...
...I NEVER HAD A DREAM ABOUT BEING CHASED BY A SPIRIT LIKE THAT.

HOW ABOUT SOMEBODY OTHER THAN YOU?
AH!

HIMAWARI-CHAN TOLD ME ABOUT A DREAM WHERE SHE WAS BEING CHASED BY SOMETHING.
BUT THAT WAS HIMAWARI-CHAN'S FIRST DREAM OF THE YEAR. IT WASN'T MY...

AND SO...
...HIMAWARI-CHAN'S DREAM BECAME A TRUE DREAM.

BUT WHY...

BECAUSE YOU BOUGHT HER DREAM.

HUH? I NEVER GAVE HIMAWARI-CHAN ANY MONEY.
ANY-THING OTHER THAN MONEY?

UM...

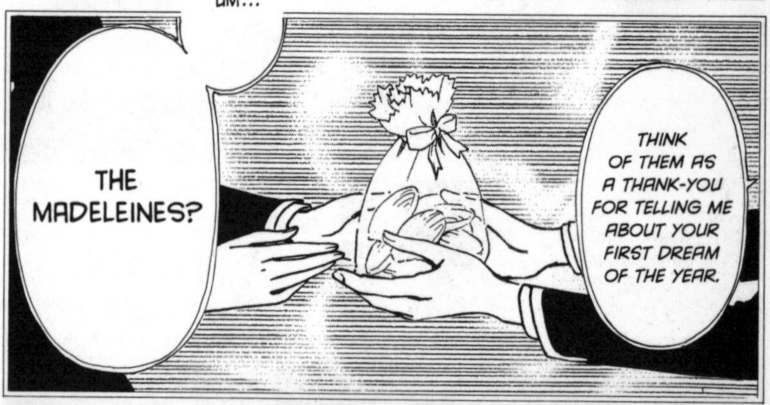
THINK OF THEM AS A THANK-YOU FOR TELLING ME ABOUT YOUR FIRST DREAM OF THE YEAR.
THE MADELEINES?

WATANUKI, YOU BECAME A DREAM BUYER.

IF YOU HEAR WHAT HAPPENS IN A DREAM AND YOU PAY A PRICE FOR IT...

...THAT DREAM BECOMES YOURS.

AND THAT DREAM TURNS INTO REALITY.

THEN... THE SPIRIT THAT WAS CHASING ME...
...WAS HIMAWARI-CHAN'S DREAM?
AND THE WHITE HORSE WITH DÔMEKI RIDING...

THAT WAS PROBABLY DÔMEKI'S DREAM.

HE WAS DÔMEKI'S GRAND-FATHER...

BE THANKFUL THAT YOU GAVE DÔMEKI SOME MADELEINES TOO.

IT WASN'T ME WHO GAVE THEM TO HIM.

THE VAST MAJORITY OF THOSE WHO BUY DREAMS ARE INTERESTED IN GOOD DREAMS.
THOSE WHO WOULD PURPOSELY BUY A NIGHT-MARE ARE... RARE.

I DIDN'T KNOW ABOUT IT!

IF I HAD KNOWN, I'D NEVER HAVE BOUGHT A DREAM OR ANYTHING WHERE A SPIRIT LIKE THAT APPEARS.
REALLY?

WOULDN'T YOU HAVE BOUGHT IT, EVEN KNOWING IT WAS A NIGHT-MARE…
…AS LONG AS IT WAS HIMAWARI-CHAN'S DREAM?
EH HEH HEH
WELL… IF IT WAS HIMAWARI-CHAN'S DREAM…
IT COULD BE A NIGHTMARE…

STARE

WHY IS THAT?
EH?

SAY, WATANUKI…
Y-YES…?
WHAT IS IT ABOUT HIMAWARI-CHAN THAT YOU LIKE SO MUCH?

WHAT...?
W-WELL, SHE'S CUTE, AND NICE...
E-EVERY-THING ABOUT HER.

REALLY?

IS THAT REALLY TRUE?

......

THEN...

WHAT IS IT ABOUT DÔMEKI THAT YOU HATE?
EVERY-THING ABOUT HIM!
QUICK ANSWER!!
DOOM

EH?
WHAT'S THAT?

I'D REALLY LIKE TO HAVE SOME STEWED EGGPLANT RIGHT NOW...
AND BEER! ♥

EGGPLANT?

WHOOSH

YOU DON'T MEAN...

DA-DOOM

MY FIRST DREAM OF THE YEAR WAS ONLY REFERRING TO THIS?!

WHY IS MY DREAM ON SUCH A TINY SCALE?!

OH, THAT'S RIGHT.
THE ARROW.

WAS THAT A TRUE DREAM TOO?! YÛKO-SAN!!
あははは
AH HA HA HA

YOU'LL HAVE TO GET THAT BOUGHT FROM YOU.

BOUGHT FROM ME...? BY WHO?

BY A DREAM BUYER.

NOW...
WHERE MIGHT ONE BE...?
?
?

MAYBE WE SHOULD LET THE ARROW FIND ONE.

SST

WA...?
FWAA

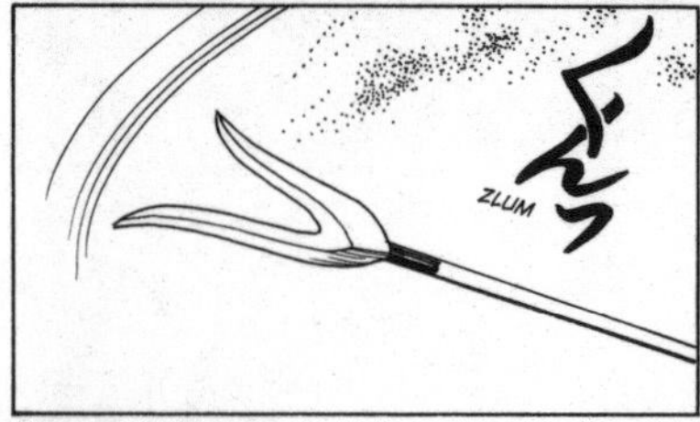
ZLUM

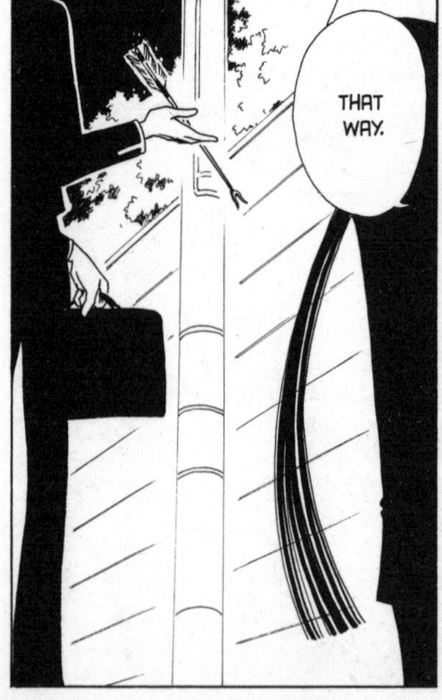
THAT WAY.

すっ
SST
EH?
ひょいっ
GWIM
YOU CAN'T GO THAT WAY.
HUH? BUT THE ARROW IS TRYING TO GO THROUGH THERE.
AND SO IT'S POINTING THE WAY THROUGH THERE.
TOO NARROW!
WHY DO I HAVE TO GO THROUGH THIS NARROW SPACE?!

THIS IS A HUGE, WIDE ROAD! WHY CAN'T I JUST GO THIS WAY?!

ZWIM

ZWIM

BECAUSE YOU *HAVE* TO GO THIS WAY!

THAT'S BECAUSE THIS IS ANOTHER WORLD.

I MEAN...
LOOK.

THERE'S ONE.

WH—
WHAT IS THAT?!

A DREAM BUYER.
ONE WHO MAKES A LIVING BY BUYING AND RAISING DREAMS.

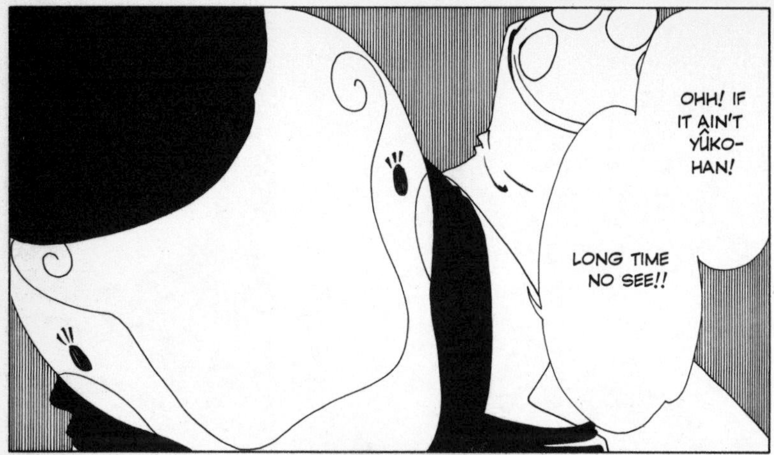
OHH! IF IT AIN'T YÛKO-HAN!
LONG TIME NO SEE!!

A-AN OSAKA ACCENT?
HOW'S BUSI-NESS?
NORMALLY I'D TELL YA THAT IT'S SO-SO, BUT...

...NOWADAYS THERE AIN'T SO MANY PEOPLE DREAMIN' THE DREAMS THAT GOT ANY WORTH!
NOTHIN' AT ALL!
HM?

HUHH?!
HEY, BROTHER! THAT THERE!

ARE YOU GONNA SELL IT TO ME?!
うる GRABBY
うる GRABBY
EH?

NO! I-I MEAN...
IT'S SORTA MINE, IT SORTA ISN'T...
YES, THE BOY BOUGHT THE DREAM.
わあっ WAA!

IS THAT *YOUR* DREAM?!

YOU GOTTA SELL ME THAT SCRAP OF DREAM!!
EH?
HUH?

GO AND TAKE A GOOD-FORTUNE DREAM FROM ME!
NO, TAKE TWO OF 'EM!
NO...
WHAT I'M SAYING—
THAT AIN'T ENOUGH FOR YOU?
URRM!
THEN, THREE!!
WHOOSH
EH? EH?

YOU'RE AN EXPERT DREAM BUYER.
YOU SHOULD KNOW EXACTLY WHAT THE DREAM ARROW IS WORTH.

IF YOU LET THIS OPPORTUNITY PASS YOU BY, YOU MAY NEVER BE ABLE TO BUY ONE LIKE IT AGAIN.

ぽん POFF

OH, NO!! A BAD, BAD PERSON IS HERE!

URRRRMM...

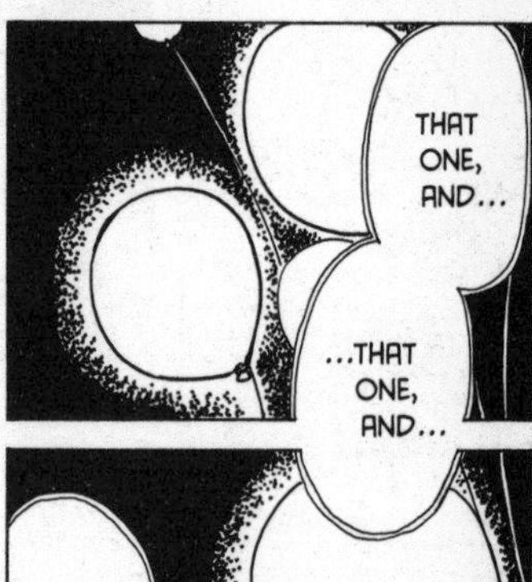

THAT ONE, AND...
...THAT ONE, AND...

...THAT!

I'VE BEEN RAISING THOSE FOREVER!
AND THAT'S THE ONLY REASON WHY THEY'RE VALUABLE ENOUGH TO BUY THE ARROW.

にっこり
SMILE
URRRRRM!!!

JUST TAKE THEM, YOU THIEF!
ぱっ
WHOOSH

UM...

ほわん
POWAAN

I JUST CAN'T COMPETE AGAINST YOU, SISTER.
WOW!

IT'S A GREAT DREAM...
...AND YOU'VE BOUGHT IT.

GWIM

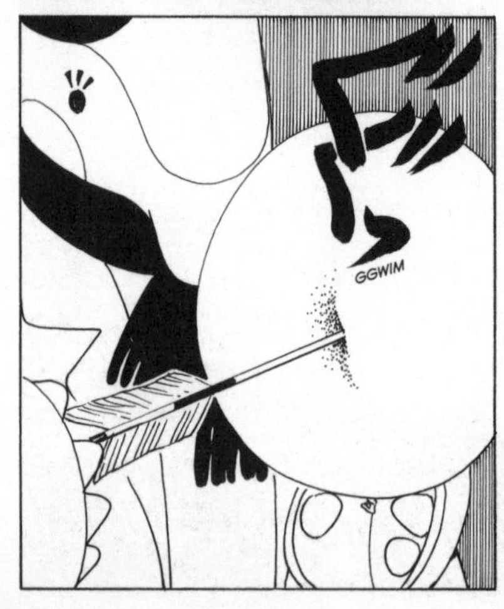
GGWIM

PAAA

WOW!

LOOK AT ALL THE LIGHT IT'S PUTTING OUT!

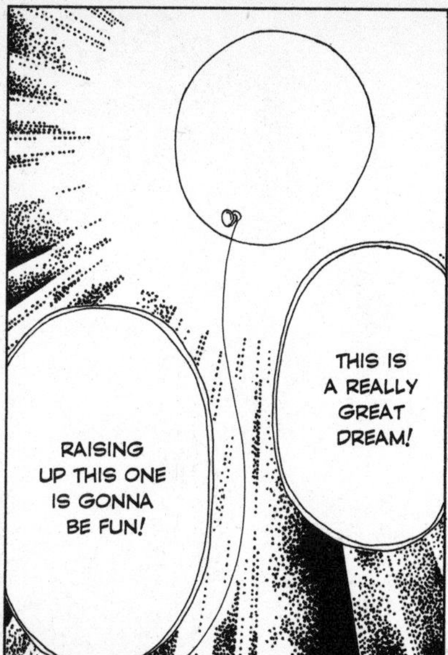

THIS IS A REALLY GREAT DREAM!
RAISING UP THIS ONE IS GONNA BE FUN!

YOU FIND FUN IN RAISING ALL OF YOUR DREAMS.

I'M SURE...

...THAT IT WILL BE ABLE TO BANISH ANY NIGHTMARE.

IT'LL BE A SACRED DREAM.

YOU CAN PUT IN ALL THE SWEET WORDS YOU WANT.
BUT I AIN'T GIVING AWAY ANY MORE.

HA HA
TOO BAD FOR ME.

I GOT MYSELF A TERRIFIC DREAM! THIS IS A GOOD DAY FOR ME!
I FEEL GOOD ENOUGH TO STOP BY THE FOX SPIRIT'S CART AND CELEBRATE WITH SOME ODEN!

YÛKO-HAN— AND YOU, BROTHER... YOU WANNA COME ALONG?
SUCH A WONDERFUL OFFER IS VERY TEMPTING, BUT...
...IT'S ABOUT TIME FOR THE PATHWAY TO THIS WORLD TO CLOSE.

THAT'S RIGHT! IF YOU DON'T GET MOVIN', YOU'LL NEVER GET BACK!
WHEN YOU TALK ABOUT THE FOX SPIRIT'S ODEN...
YOU'RE TALKING ABOUT AN ADULT WITH A CHILD?

YEAH. YOU KNOW 'EM, BROTHER?
I'VE EATEN AT THEIR CART BEFORE, AND ALSO...
...AT THE HYAKKI YAKÔ PROCESSION...

COULD YOU PLEASE GIVE THIS TO THE YOUNG BOY FOX SPIRIT?

IT'S A THANK-YOU FOR WHEN HE SAVED ME AT THE HYAKKI YAKÔ.

ぱちくり
BLINK BLINK
A HUMAN THANKING A FOX SPIRIT?

IS THAT A BAD GIFT TO USE AS A THANK-YOU?

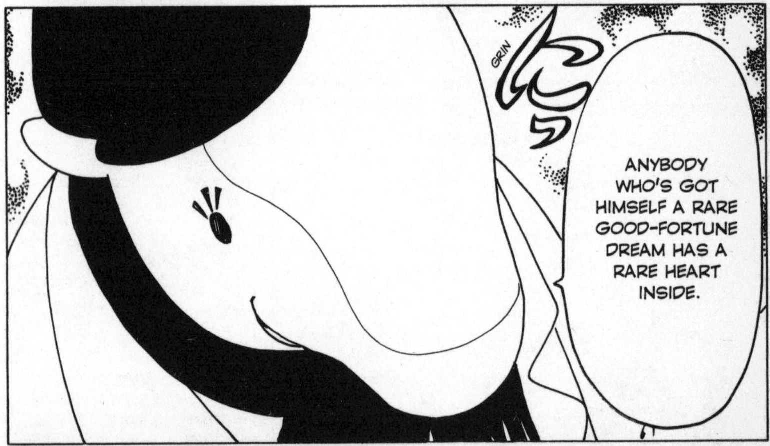
にっ
GRIN
ANYBODY WHO'S GOT HIMSELF A RARE GOOD-FORTUNE DREAM HAS A RARE HEART INSIDE.

?
?

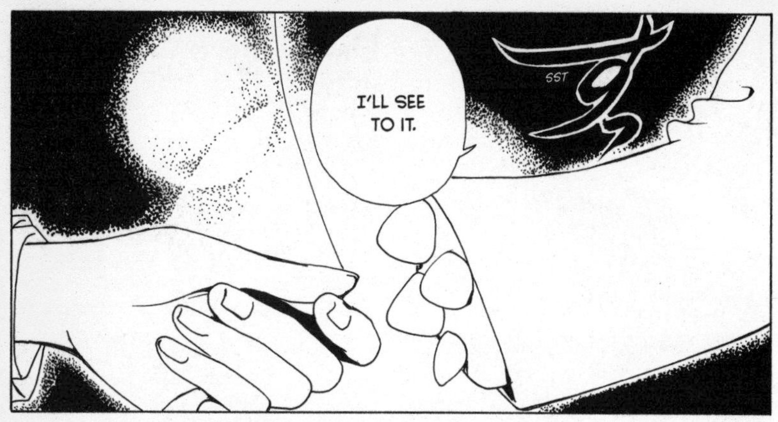

I'LL BE SURE TO PASS IT ON TO THE ODEN CART OWNER'S KID, SO DON'T YOU FRET.

FWAA

AH...

OKAY.

OKAY THEN...
GOOD BYE!

YOU MEAN WE HAVE TO GO BETWEEN THAT POLE AND WALL AGAIN?
NOW... SHALL WE GO BACK OURSELVES?
TO THE REAL WORLD?

NO.
THIS TIME IT'S HERE.
GRIN
THAT'S IMPOSSIBLE!!

THAT WAS AN AWFUL EXPERIENCE!
NOT EVEN A CAT COULD GET THROUGH THERE!
AND IN THE END, I HAD TO GIVE YÛKO-SAN THREE BALLOONS!
I GUESS IT WAS YÛKO-SAN DOING THE BARGAINING, THOUGH.

MAN, I'M TIRED!
AND SHE SAID SHE WANTS ME TO MAKE BREAKFAST FOR HER.
BETTER GET TO SLEEP...
POP

WHOOSH

DÔMEKI!

WHAT ARE YOU DOING HERE?!

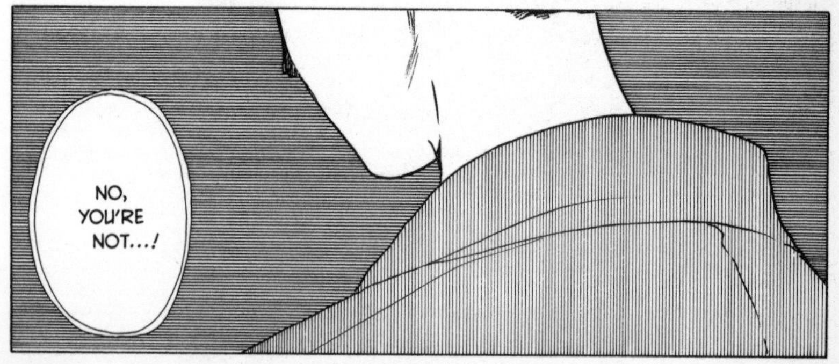

YOU'RE...
...DÔMEKI'S GRAND-FATHER...?!

YOU'RE HAVING TROUBLE DEALING WITH SHIZUKA?
SHIZUKA?
AH! THAT'S DÔMEKI'S NAME?

TROUBLE DEALING WITH HIM...?
MAYBE I JUST DON'T GET THE GUY.

THE MOMENT WE FIRST MET, IT TURNED INTO A BIG FIGHT.
AND SINCE THEN HIS ATTITUDE HAS BEEN TERRIBLE.
BUT ALL THE WHILE, WE SEEM TO KEEP GETTING CAUGHT UP IN EACH OTHER'S BUSINESS.

LIKE WITH THIS EYE...

THAT WAS THE BOY'S CHOICE.

BUT...IF ANY-BODY DOES SOMETHING THAT CAN'T BE UNDONE, AND DOES IT FOR MY SAKE...
...I JUST HATE THAT.

SHIZUKA IS A VERY STRONG BOY.
SST
AFTER ALL, WHEN HE WAS A CHILD...

!?
SST
EHH?!
BLAMM

xxxHOLiC
～×××ホリック～

ぱち
BLAMM

EH?
EH?
ガバ
GAMPH
WHAT WAS...
がら
RATTLE
A DREAM.

STILL... ON THE OTHER HAND...
WHY A DREAM ABOUT DÔMEKI'S GRANDFATHER?

AH. THAT NIGHT WHEN I WAS BEING CHASED BY THE SPIRIT, I REMEMBER BEING RESCUED BY HIM AND...
ぽん
POFF
I DON'T MEAN THAT.

YOU HAD THE DREAM THAT WAS IN THIS BALLOON, RIGHT?

HUH?
THE DREAM INSIDE THIS BROKEN BALLOON—THE GOOD-FORTUNE DREAM YOU BOUGHT AFTER THE DREAM BUYER RAISED IT FOR A LONG TIME WAS A DREAM OF DÔMEKI'S GRANDFATHER.

A COINCI-DENCE LIKE THAT...

THERE IS NO COINCIDENCE IN THIS WORLD.
WHAT THERE IS...

...IS HITSUZEN.

THEN WHAT I JUST DREAMED WAS ALSO...
WHAT KIND OF DREAM WAS IT?

HE SHOWED ME A PHOTO.

DÔMEKI'S GRAND-FATHER...
...SAID THAT DÔMEKI IS A STRONG BOY.
THEN HE SHOWED ME A PICTURE OF A GIRL IN A KIMONO.

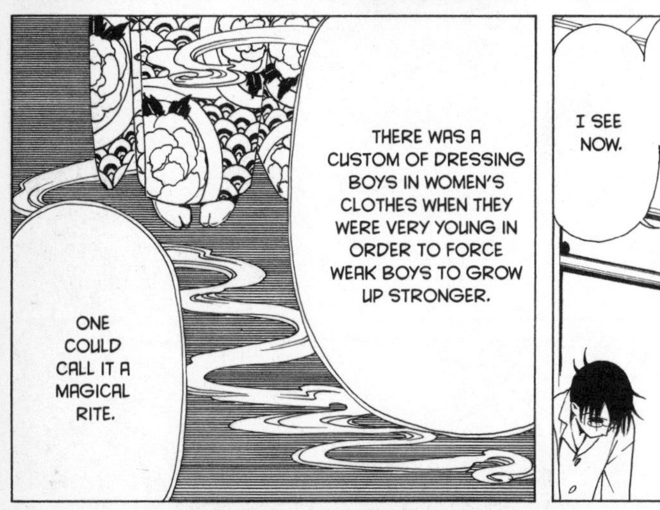
AH...
I SEE NOW.
THERE WAS A CUSTOM OF DRESSING BOYS IN WOMEN'S CLOTHES WHEN THEY WERE VERY YOUNG IN ORDER TO FORCE WEAK BOYS TO GROW UP STRONGER.
ONE COULD CALL IT A MAGICAL RITE.

THEN THAT MEANS...
...THAT THE PHOTO THAT I SAW WAS...

DÔMEKI WHEN HE WAS A LITTLE KID!!!
うっしゃっ
YEAH!!

THE PICTURE!
WHERE IS THE PHOTO?!
ばばっ!
WHOOSH WHOOSH WHOOSH
きょろきょろ
GLANCE GLANCE
I DOUBT IT EXISTS.

EHH?!
DID YOU TAKE THE PHOTO IN THE DREAM?

NO.
BEFORE I COULD, I WOKE UP.

THEN IT'S GONE.
DAMMIT!!
がくっ
SLUMP
BUT... BUT...
NOW I KNOW PART OF DÔMEKI'S MOST EMBARRASSING PAST!
よし!
YES!

はああああ
PAAAA
THEY DRESSED HIM AS A GIRL WHEN HE WAS A KID!!
I'VE SEIZED UPON MR. IRON-MASK-FACE'S WEAKNESS!!
YOU FINALLY GET YOURSELF A GOOD OMEN, AND YOU USE IT *THIS* WAY TO MAKE YOURSELF HAPPY.
IN A MANNER OF SPEAKING, YOU *ARE* A RARE BEING, WATANUKI.
ぐっ
POIT
あーははは
BWA HA HA HA HA

WHEN I WORE A KIMONO?

MY GRAND-FATHER TOLD ME TO.

HOW DID YOU KNOW ABOUT IT?

ZWAMMM

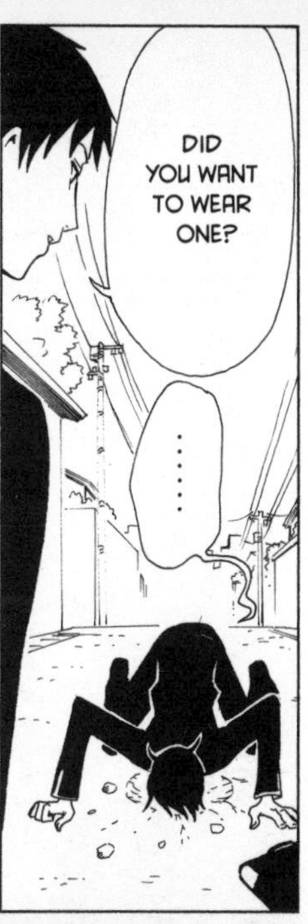
DID YOU WANT TO WEAR ONE?
......

WHO SAID HE WANTS TO WEAR ONE?!
GWAA

AAAAH! HE WAS NEVER GIVEN THE SENSE OF SHAME THAT'S GIVEN TO THE NORMAL HUMAN, AND THAT'S WHAT MAKES HIM AN IDIOT!!
WHAT'S WITH HIM THIS EARLY IN THE MORNING?

ZUWUMP

UGWAH!

にっ
HEH
YÛKO SAID SHE WANTS YOU TO COOK SOMETHING WITH THESE EGGPLANTS.

IT'S A DINNER PARTY!
んあ
HM?

ん
AAN

ばや
BYAA

ふら～
FLUU
MY...
...FIRST DREAM OF THE YEAR...
...WAS JUST ABOUT THAT...
WHUMP
ばたっ
STEWED EGGPLANT!
EGG-PLANT WITH CHEESE ON TOP!

EGGPLANT AU GRATIN!
EGGPLANT DENGAKU!
WHISPER
FRIED EGG-PLANT...
TWIRL
くる
TWIRL
くる

xxxHOLiC
〜×××ホリック〜

ひらり
FLIF

THE CHERRY TREES ON THE SCHOOL GROUNDS ARE BEAUTIFUL THIS YEAR, TOO!
YOU'RE RIGHT!

IT'S TURNED COMPLETELY INTO SPRING, HUH?
ZWANNG
OHH!

MUNCH
MUNCH
THAT'S SO TRUE!
MY HEART HAS TURNED COMPLETELY INTO SPRING, TOO!

OH, YEAH!
DID YOU SEE THAT TV PROGRAM LAST NIGHT AT NINE?
HM?
WHAT PROGRAM WAS THAT?
"TRUE STORIES! GHOSTLY EXPERIENCES. A WORLD YOU MAY NOT KNOW ABOUT."

I-I DIDN'T SEE IT.
I MISSED IT, TOO.

IT HAD A STORY ABOUT A WOMAN WHO SAID SHE SAW A GHOST IN AN OLD SHUT-DOWN HOTEL.
MOST OF THE SHOW WAS ABOUT HOW THEY TRIED TO EXORCISE THE GHOST.
THERE WAS THIS GIRL THEY CALLED A "SPIRITUAL PSYCHIC," I THINK.
THE GIRL WHO DID THE EXORCISM WAS SOMEWHERE AROUND GRADE-SCHOOL AGE. I WAS SO SURPRISED.
R-REALLY...?

THEY'RE STILL DOING IT!
NEXT TIME IT'LL BE A GHOST THAT'S HAUNTING A CHERRY-BLOSSOM TREE.

YEAH! I LOVE IT!
I-IS THAT SO...?

I-INTERESTING...

HIMAWARI-CHAN, YOU HAVE NO PROBLEMS WITH THAT SUPERNATURAL OR SCARY STUFF, HUH?

HIMAWARI-SAN...

BUT I SUPPOSE IT WOULD BE VERY HARD ON THOSE PEOPLE WHO CAN ACTUALLY SEE OR FEEL THEM.

MUNCH
もぎゅ
MUNCH
もぎゅ
MUNCH
もぎゅ
MUNCH
もぎゅ
MUNCH
もぎゅ

LISTEN! WHEN A GUY'S BEING MOVED BY THE KINDNESS OF OTHERS, DON'T SPOIL THE MOOD WITH YOUR LOUD EATING!!
MUNCH?
もぎゅ?

私立十字学園

MAN, THAT DÔMEKI IS SUCH A JERK!!
NOT ONLY DOES HE HAVE NO SHAME, HE'S ALSO LACKING IN DELICACY!

BUT DÔMEKI-KUN SURE LOOKED LIKE HE WAS ENJOYING THE FOOD.
HE WAS OVER-EATING!

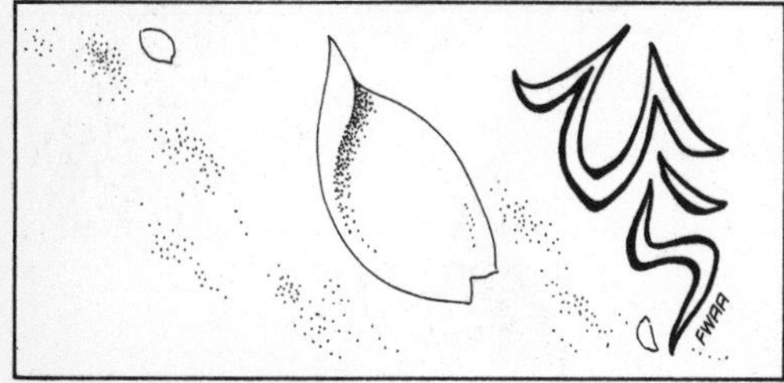
FWAA

WOW!
WHAT A HUGE TREE!
THERE ARE CHERRY BLOSSOMS BLOOMING HERE TOO, HUH?

......
YOU'RE...

TMP
YOU STAY AWAY FROM HER!

DON'T YOU GET NEAR HER!
EH?
NO...
UM...

YOU SAW HER ON TELE-VISION?!
SO YOU KNOW ALL ABOUT IT, HUH?
IF ANY-BODY TOUCHES HER, SHE LOSES SOME OF HER POWER!

HONESTLY! I CAN'T TAKE MY EYES OFF OF YOU FOR A SECOND!

I REALLY *WISH* YOU WOULD STAY AWAY FROM PEOPLE WHO DON'T UNDERSTAND YOUR SITUATION!

I GUESS THIS TIME IT CAN'T BE HELPED BECAUSE OF THE PLACE WE'RE IN...

?

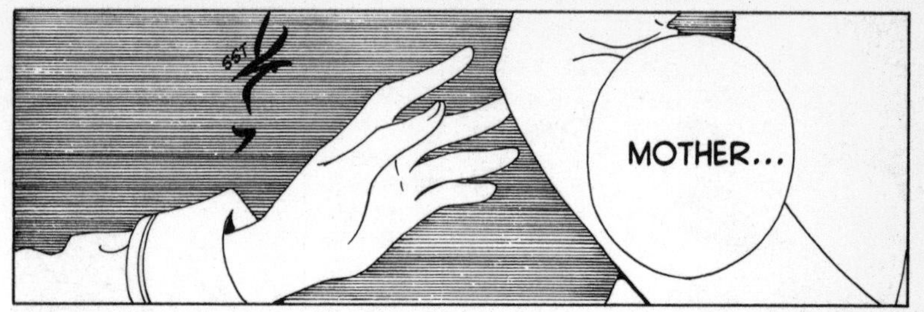
SST
MOTHER...

WHOOSH

......
AH...

......

AH...
AHH...
WHAT?
WHAT'S
WRONG?
DON'T
YOU THINK
IT'S TIME WE
WENT HOME?
HUH?

YOU DO UNDERSTAND MY SITUATION AT LEAST A LITTLE, DON'T YOU?

EH...?

WATANUKI-KUN, ARE YOU ALL RIGHT?
たた
TMP TMP
Y-YEAH...

SHE'S THE SPIRITUAL PSYCHIC I SAW ON TELEVISION LAST NIGHT...

xxxHOLiC
~×××ホリック~

A SPIRITUAL PSYCHIC... HUH?

SHE WAS A GIRL.
STILL VERY YOUNG.
AND THIS GIRL SAID THAT TO YOU?

"YOU *DO* UNDERSTAND MY SITUATION AT LEAST A LITTLE, DON'T YOU?"
..... YES.

WHAT DID YOU THINK OF IT, WATANUKI?

I DON'T KNOW ANY-THING ABOUT EXORCISING GHOSTS OR ANYTHING LIKE THAT...
BUT...

I HAD THE FEELING THAT SHE WAS SOMETHING LIKE ME.

......
SOMETHING LIKE...HM?

WHICH MEANING DO YOU MEAN?
WHEN YOU SAY "WHICH"...?

......

EITHER WAY, YOU AND THAT GIRL HAVE A CONNECTION NOW.

WATANUKI! THE BATH IS READY!
AH!
THANKS! I'LL BE RIGHT THERE!

I'LL GO GET YOU REFILLS OF SOME FRESH-BREWED TEA.
SST

THAT IS ALSO WATANUKI'S CHOICE.

さあああああ
SHHHHHH
私立十字学園
CROSS PRIVATE SCHOOL

HIMAWARI-CHAN CAN'T COME SINCE SHE'S HELPING OUT THE TEACHER TODAY.

AWW! MY FUN LUNCH-BREAK BENTO TIME HAS TO BE SPENT WITH YOU!
THE LETDOWN HAS LEFT ME COMPLETELY DEPRESSED!
HUH? YOU'RE EATING ALREADY?!
EVEN BEFORE ME, THE GUY WHO MADE IT?
ぱく
MUNCH

GLANCE

むっ
GRR
WHAT?!

YESTERDAY I SAW A LITTLE GIRL BENEATH A CHERRY TREE...
...WITH THIS EYE.

WHAT KIND OF RULES DOES THIS EYE PLAY BY?

YOU DON'T ALWAYS SEE THROUGH IT, RIGHT?
RIGHT.

BUT WHEN THE RAIJÛ WAS THERE, YOU SAW IT.

THAT WOULD MEAN THAT YOU CAN SEE WHEN SOMETHING VERY UNUSUAL APPEARS, HUH?
LIKE SPIRITS OR MONSTERS...
ACCORDING TO HIMAWARI-CHAN, THE GIRL HAS HAD SOME ODD EXPERIENCES...

BUT WHEN I HAD THAT DREAM ABOUT YOUR GRANDFATHER, YOU DIDN'T SEE IT, DID YOU?
I DON'T THINK YOU SEE DREAMS WITH YOUR EYES.

OH, MAYBE SO...
THAT MAKES SENSE.
もぐもぐ
MUNCH MUNCH

BUT YOU DON'T SEE *EVERYTHING* THAT'S STRANGE, DO YOU?
THE SPIRIT I SAW ON THE WAY HOME FROM SCHOOL LAST WEEK...
YOU DIDN'T SAY ANYTHING ABOUT IT THE NEXT DAY.

I DIDN'T SEE ANY-THING.
IF SO...
THEN THE SIZE OR STRENGTH OF THE SPIRIT MAY...
WHAT HAPPENED WHEN YOU SAW THAT SPIRIT LAST WEEK?

WELL... IT WAS JUST A LITTLE THING.
SO I JUST KEPT ON GOING.
IT WASN'T ANYTHING TO BE SHOCKED AT.

IF THAT'S TRUE...

...THEN ONE MORE CONDITION MAY BE YOU YOURSELF.

YOU EXPERIENCED THE STRANGE THING THAT KUNOGI TALKED ABOUT.

AT THE TIME, YOUR FEELINGS WERE HEAVILY AFFECTED, AND MAYBE THAT'S WHEN I WAS ABLE TO SEE.

Y-YOU THINK SO?
IT'S BETTER THAN YOU BEING ABLE TO SEE THROUGH IT 24 HOURS A DAY, BUT I STILL DON'T GET WHAT'S GOING ON.
I CAN'T SEE ANYTHING THAT YOU SEE, SO IT FEELS LIKE I'M AT A DISADVANTAGE.

THAT GIRL...

SHE'S HUMAN.

REMEMBER THAT GHOST-STORY TV SHOW, THAT HIMAWARI-CHAN WAS TALKING ABOUT?
THE GIRL I MET WAS THE SPIRITUAL PSYCHIC.

THAT MEANS...

...SINCE I SAW IT THROUGH THAT EYE, THEN THAT GIRL'S POWERS MUST BE REAL.

私立十字学園
CROSS

IT'S BEEN RAINING EVER SINCE MORNING...

I HOPE THE CHERRY TREES DON'T LOSE ALL OF THEIR BLOSSOMS.

THIS IS WHERE I SAW THE GIRL YESTERDAY.
さあああ
SHHHHH
!?

PLASH
PLASH
IF YOU KEEP STANDING THERE...
...YOU'LL CATCH COLD!

......
I KNEW WE'D MEET AGAIN.
......
EH?

WHEN YOU SAY THAT, YOU MEAN THAT YOU FORESAW US MEETING HERE?

NO, NOT THAT.

I WAS THINKING THAT I'D LIKE TO SEE YOU AGAIN.

A LONG TIME AGO, MY MOTHER SAID...
...THAT IF I WANT SOMETHING TO HAPPEN, I SHOULD KEEP THINKING ABOUT IT, AND IT WILL HAPPEN.
SO I THOUGHT THAT I WANTED TO SEE YOU AGAIN.

SEE ME?
YES.
WHY?
BECAUSE WE'RE LIKE EACH OTHER.
ZATT

YOU THOUGHT SO TOO, RIGHT?
WHEN WE FIRST MET.
YEAH...
SO YOU KNOW, DON'T YOU?
..... YEAH.

THAT WOMAN UP THERE.

SHE'S FROM A LONG TIME AGO.
SHE'S THE GHOST OF THE HAUNTED CHERRY TREE THEY WERE TALKING ABOUT ON TV, HUH?

I THINK IT'S HER.
BUT IT ISN'T AS IF SHE'S THREATENING ANYBODY. SHE'S JUST HERE BECAUSE SHE LOVES THE TREE.

I THINK YOU'RE RIGHT.

AND SHE SAYS IF SHE'S A BOTHER, SHE'LL DISAPPEAR.

WITH ALL OF THOSE PEOPLE FROM TV COMING...

...SHE FEELS SORRY FOR THE CHERRY TREE.

BUT...
...IF THAT WOMAN WERE TO DISAPPEAR...
...THE CHERRY TREE WOULD WITHER AND DIE.
THE TREE HAS LIVED OUT ITS LIFESPAN. IT'S ONLY BLOOMING BECAUSE SHE'S THERE.

IF I HAD NEVER COME HERE, THAT WOMAN WOULD HAVE STAYED IN THE TREE FOREVER.
AND THE TREE WOULD HAVE CONTINUED TO BLOOM.

ME TOO. THAT'S WHAT I WAS THINKING...

AND NOW?

I'D LIKE TO KEEP IT FROM ENDING THAT WAY...
...I'M WONDERING IF THERE IS SOMETHING I CAN DO TO HELP.

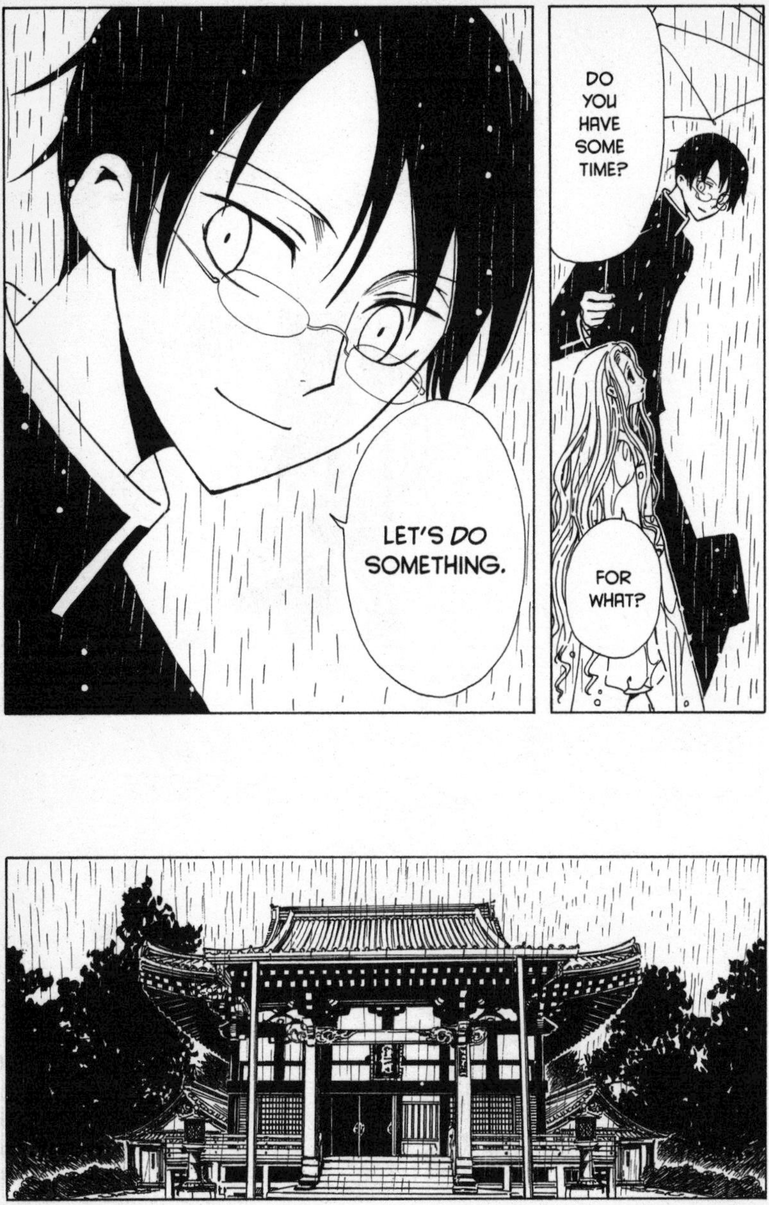

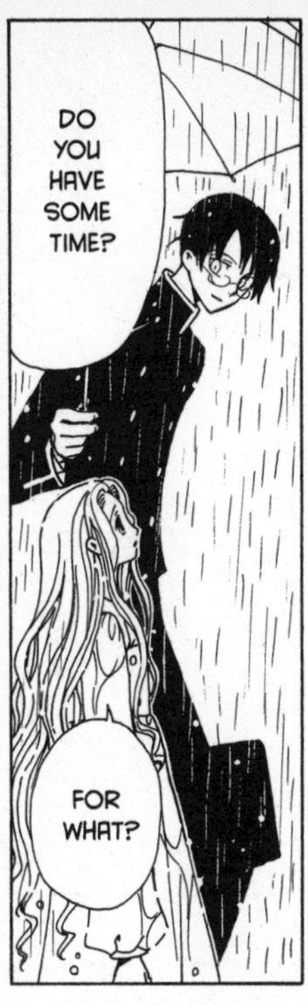
DO YOU HAVE SOME TIME?
FOR WHAT?

LET'S *DO* SOMETHING.

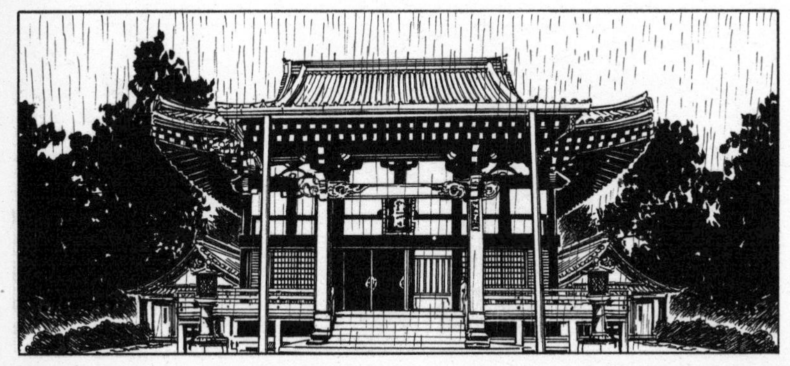

THAT'S A TEMPLE.
IT'S WHERE A REALLY IRRITATING GUY LIVES.
BUT HE'S SAID THAT IT'S A PURE PLACE.

SHE LIKES IT.
GOOD.
THAT CHERRY TREE MAY WITHER AND DIE, BUT...
...SHE FOUND A NEW PLACE TO BE.

......
YES...

I'M GOING HOME.
BEFORE MOTHER COMES TO GET ME.

SORRY.
I TOOK YOU ALL THIS WAY IN THE RAIN.
IT'S OKAY.

HERE.
I'M ALREADY SOAKED, AND IT ISN'T TOO COLD TODAY.
TRUE...
BUT I'M ALREADY SOAKED, TOO.

BE-SIDES...

WE'LL BE ABLE TO MEET AGAIN WHEN YOU RETURN IT TO ME.

YOUR NAME!
TELL ME YOUR NAME.
I DON'T WANT TO JUST KEEP SAYING "YOU." I WANT TO CALL YOU BY NAME.

KOHANE TSUYURI.
HOW IS THAT SPELLED?
TSUYURI IS SPELLED WITH THE CHARACTERS FOR MAY 7TH.

I'M CALLED KIMIHIRO WATANUKI.
WATANUKI IS SPELLED WITH THE CHARACTERS FOR APRIL 1ST.
THEY'RE LIKE EACH OTHER.
AND YOUR PERSONAL NAME?
THE CHARAC-TERS FOR SMALL FEATHERS.
WHAT A PRETTY NAME!
......

DO YOU MIND IF I CALL YOU KOHANE-CHAN?
KOHANE...
...CHAN?

OH! WE JUST MET, SO YOU DON'T WANT ME TO USE -CHAN ON YOUR NAME, RIGHT?

ふる
SHAKE SHAKE

IT'S BEEN A LONG TIME SINCE I'VE BEEN CALLED THAT.
I MEAN...
...IT'S BEEN A LONG TIME SINCE ANYONE'S CALLED ME BY NAME.

SEE YOU
LATER,
KOHANE-
CHAN!

......
SEE
YOU...

THEY SAY
THAT FOOLS
NEVER CATCH
COLDS, BUT...

I THINK THAT *IDIOTS* CAN CATCH THEM.

WHO ARE YOU CALLING AN IDIOT?

......

......
IDIOT.

DRINK THIS.
WHAT IS IT?
IT'S CALLED SHÔGAYU.
MY GRAND-FATHER WOULD OFTEN MAKE THIS ON COLD DAYS.
HMM...
OH, YEAH.
IN THAT TREE...
THE WOMAN IN THE KIMONO?
I'LL READ THE SUTRAS FOR HER AFTER-WARD.
YOU CAN DO THAT?
IT'LL BE JUST GOING THROUGH THE MOTIONS.

BUT...
...YOU WERE ABLE TO SEE THROUGH THE EYE AGAIN?

I CAN STILL SEE HER.

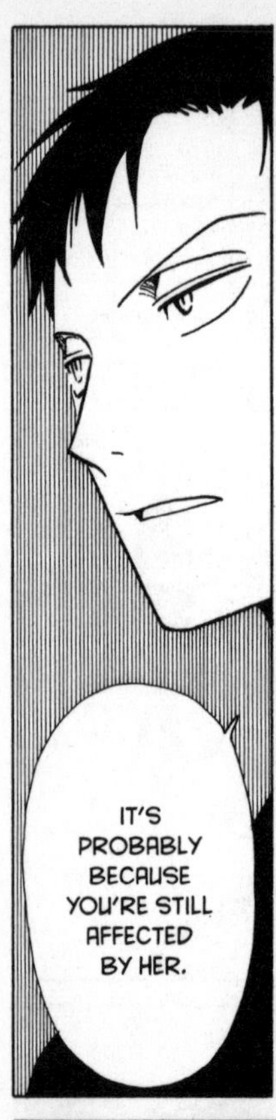
IT'S PROBABLY BECAUSE YOU'RE STILL AFFECTED BY HER.

DÔMEKI...
WHAT DOES YOUR FAMILY NORMALLY CALL YOU?

SHIZUKA.

YOUR FIRST NAME. ME TOO. WHEN MY PARENTS WERE ALIVE, THEY CALLED ME KIMIHIRO.

KOHANE-CHAN SAID THAT IT HAD BEEN A LONG TIME SINCE SHE WAS CALLED BY NAME...

HER MOTHER WAS RIGHT WITH HER. FOR IT TO BE A LONG TIME...

カタン
KA-TANK
ばん
WHOOSH
WHERE HAVE YOU BEEN?!
ON A RAINY DAY LIKE THIS? WHAT WOULD WE DO IF YOU CAUGHT A COLD?!
THE TELEVISION CREW IS GOING TO RECORD TOMORROW!
IF THEY HAVE TO CANCEL IT...!
....

I WENT TO WHERE THE CHERRY TREE IS.
THE CHERRY...
AH... THAT'S WHERE THEY'RE GOING TO DO THE RECORDING.
GASP

THEN WE'LL BOTH GO TOGETHER...

NOT TOGETHER.
EH?

MOTHER, YOU AND I ARE NOT TOGETHER.

YOU JUST HAPPEN TO BE HERE.

HELLO?
OH!
WE'LL BE RECORDING TOMORROW, RIGHT?
OF COURSE WE'RE PREPARED.
ABSO-LUTELY, THE EXORCISM IS REAL!
WHAT'S THAT QUESTION SUPPOSED TO MEAN?
OF COURSE IT IS!
I'VE DONE EVERYTHING TO BE SURE THAT NO IMPURITIES TOUCH HER IN ORDER TO PROTECT HER POWERS!
NOTHING IMPURE PASSES HER LIPS, EITHER!!

THE FOOD WE FEED HER IS THE SAME PURIFIED COOKING THEY HAVE AT THE TEMPLES!
NOW, ABOUT OUR PAY FOR HER APPEARANCE...

WHAT?! THAT ISN'T WHAT YOU SAID BEFORE!
とん TMP
とん TMP
とん TMP
OUR FEES SHOULD BE DOUBLE THAT!!
KACHIK

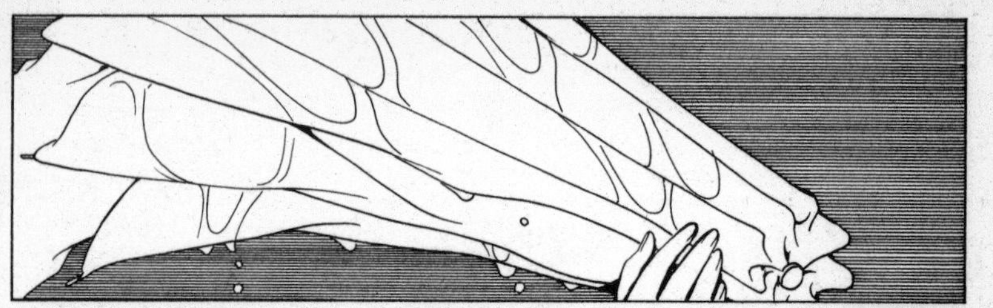

GWMM

xxxHolic
~×××ホリック~

ざあああ
SHHHH

YÛKO-SAN...

WHAT'S THE MATTER... STANDING OUT HERE WITHOUT AN UM-BRELLA.
YOU MUST BE SOAKING...

......
...DRY?

I'M WAITING.

FOR WHO?

THOSE CLOTHES...
...YOU'VE WORN THEM BEFORE...

KEE
EE
EE
EE

STEP BACK.
Y—
YES...

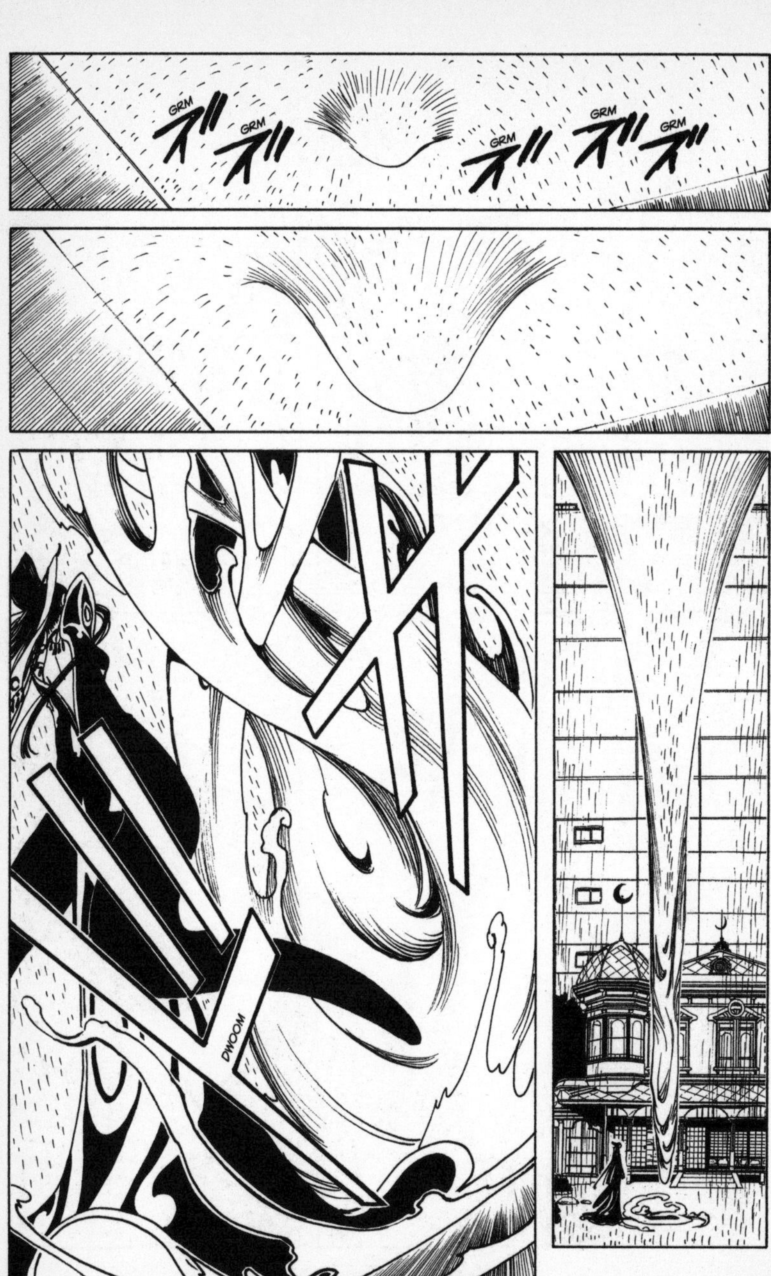
GRM
ズ
GRM
ズ
GRM
ズ
GRM
ズ
GRM
ズ
DWOOM

SO YOU'RE HERE.
SYAORAN-KUN?!
......
NO HE ISN'T!

WHAT IS YOUR WISH?
TO BE SENT TO MY RIGHT EYE.

YOUR PRICE...

I'VE ALREADY RECEIVED IT, HAVEN'T I?

EH?!

THEN YOU MAY...
...CONSIDER YOUR WISH GRANTED.
SST

ふわん
FUWAAN

SHULOOM

JUST NOW... THAT WASN'T SYAORAN-KUN, RIGHT?
ONE COULD SAY THAT HE WAS...
STILL, ONE COULD ALSO SAY HE WASN'T.

BUT DOESN'T THAT MEAN THAT SYAORAN AND HIS GROUP WILL BE IN TROUBLE?

EVEN IF THEY ARE...
...I'M LIMITED IN WHAT I CAN DO.

INSTEAD OF REGRET-TING WHAT WE CANNOT DO...
...IT IS BETTER TO DO WHAT ONE CAN.
EVEN IF, FOR EXAMPLE, WHAT YOU DO HAS NOTHING TO DO WITH THE RESULTS...

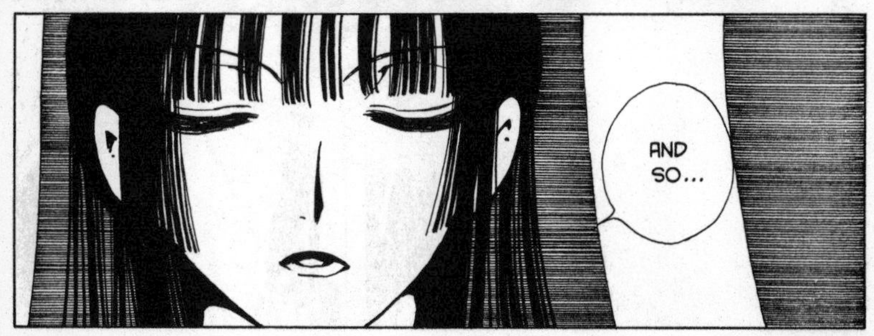

I STOPPED OVER AT A TEMPLE! WHAT ABOUT THAT IS "NO GOOD"?!

SUBAMM

NO GOOD! NO GOOD! ♥

NO GOOD! NO GOOD!

HAHH...

I THINK I'M HUNGRY.

WATANUKI, BEER.

BEER!!
BEER! ♥ BEER! ♥
ZZGL
ZZGL
BARLEY, RICE AND POTATOES ALL ABSORB LIQUIDS, YOU KNOW! ♥
WHAT IS THIS? PEOPLE DON'T CONSIDER BEER TO BE FOOD!
YOU SAID YOU WERE HUNGRY, RIGHT?

I'LL GET YOU YOUR BEER, BUT YOU'RE GOING TO EAT SOME FOOD WITH IT, UNDERSTAND?

YOU'RE GOING TO RUIN YOUR STOMACH AND LIVER AT THE SAME TIME!!

SO YOU'RE FEELING GOOD?
EH?
.....

SHFFL
SHFFL

YEAH...
THANK YOU.

IT'S TRUE. WITH KOHANE-CHAN...
...EVEN IF NOBODY ELSE CALLS HER BY NAME, I CAN.

THE THING I WANT KOHANE-CHAN TO RECEIVE IS SOMETHING I CAN GIVE.

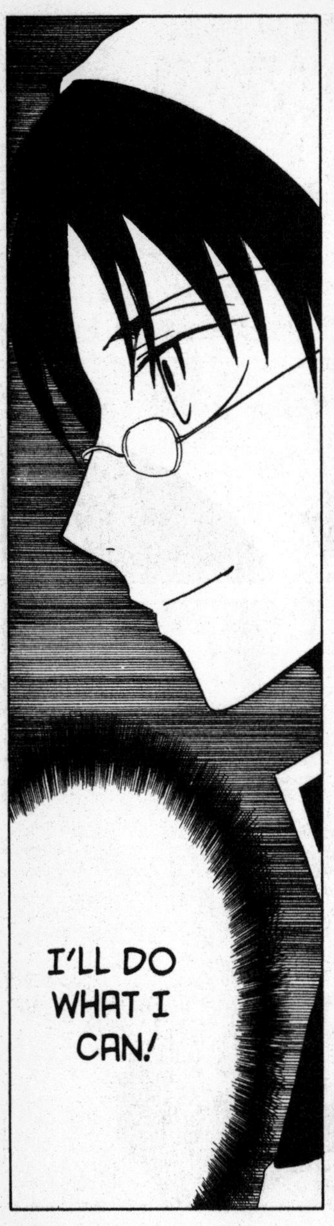
I'LL DO WHAT I CAN!

LET US BELIEVE...

...IN THE FUTURE...

...IN THOSE CHILDREN.

xxxHOLiC
～×××ホリック～

IT'S SPRING...

IT'S SPRING!

YES, IT *IS* SPRING.
THIS AFTERNOON IS BRISK AND REFRESHING.

AND THAT'S WHY I ASK...

WHY DO WE HAVE TO GET TOGETHER AT DÔMEKI'S HOUSE?!
AND WHY DO WE HAVE TO PLAY MAHJONG?!
AND WHY OUT-SIDE?!

IT ISN'T SO BAD! IT'S SUCH A BEAUTIFUL DAY!
IF YOU STAY ANGRY, YOUR ODD REACTIONS WILL GET EVEN MORE ODD.
IT ISN'T JUST HIS REACTIONS THAT ARE ODD.
YOU HAVE NO RIGHT TO TALK!
SWIK!
BESIDES, HERE...
EVERY-THING IS READY!
THEN LET'S BEGIN.

I... DON'T KNOW HOW TO PLAY MAHJONG.
SHUKA
SLUMP
OH, DON'T YOU?

IT DOESN'T MATTER. JUST HURRY UP AND XIPAI!
XI...?
SHUKA
SHUFFLE! SHUFFLE THEM UP!

ALL I GOTTA DO IS MIX THEM UP, RIGHT?
ALL RIGHT, I'LL DO IT!
SHUKA

EH...?

SHE'S HAPPY.
SHUKA

SHUKA
YOU CAN SEE HER?
YUP!
SHUKA

THE SOUND OF SHUFFLING MAHJONG TILES IS A GOOD OMEN!
SHUKA
SHUKA

THERE ARE PARTS OF CHINA WHERE IT IS THE CUSTOM TO PLAY MAHJONG AT THE TIME OF A FUNERAL.

THE SOUND IS A FAREWELL GIFT TO THE RECENTLY DEPARTED.

SHUKA

REALLY?

SHUKA

NOW...
JUST AT THE POINT WHERE OUR TILES HAVE BEEN DEALT...
HEH HEH

TEN HO!! ♥

DOOM

YÛKO, THAT'S GOOD PLAY!
MM...
HUH?

IT'S TURNING A HAND AT THE TIME A HAND IS DEALT.
IF IT'S "OYA," THEN IT'S TEN HO. IF IT'S "KO," THEN IT'S CHI HO.
HUHH?

THIS FEELS WONDER-FUL!
I GET THE FEELING THAT I HAVE AKAGI-TAN, TETSUYA-KUN, AND AKINA-CHAN JUST BEHIND WATCHING OVER ME! ♥
PAAA

WHO ARE THEY? FRIENDS OF YOURS?
SHUKA
SHUKA
AKÛKAN ZEPPÔ! SEIKYÔ MAHJONG! WAREME DE PON!
NOW! LET'S REALLY GET INTO IT!

DOOOM
MOKONA HAS A DAISHARIN! ♥
EH?
FWAP

A CHINITSU WITH DORA 10! ♥
D-DOOOM
AH?

DÔMEKI-KUN! YOU'RE TOO SOUR!
BUT...
WHAT'S GOING ON? ARE YOU ALL CHANTING SOME MYSTERIOUS SPELLS?
SHUKA
SHUKA
SHUKA

DOOM
SHÔSÛSHI!! ♥
EE?

ZWAM
NAGASHI-MANGAN!

AND...
WHILE I WAS STUCK NOT DOING ANYTHING, I WAS THE BIG LOSER!
SLUMMP
WHAT DO THEY CALL THAT IN MAHJONG JARGON?
BUTTOBI!!*

*BUTTOBI = ZERO-POINT LOSER.

I *TOLD* YOU ALL THAT I DIDN'T KNOW HOW TO PLAY MAHJONG!

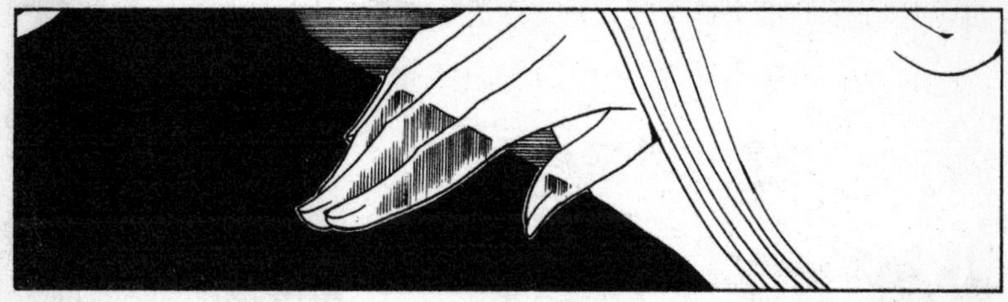

AH...
......
SHE VANISHED...

THERE WAS A PLACE SHE HAD TO GO.
AND SHE DECIDED TO GO THERE.

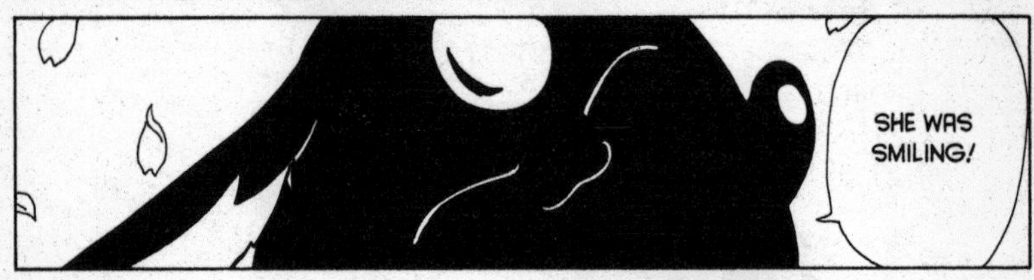

……

SO...
TUMP

A LOSER IS A LOSER.
THE WORLD OF COMPETITION IS A HARD ONE, HIROMI!
WHO'RE YOU CALLING HIROMI?!
BUT... I DON'T HAVE ANY MONEY!

VERY WELL THEN, STRIP!!

EYAAAAAAAH?!
IT'S STRIP-MAH-JONG!
YAY!

IT WAS A JOKE.
MAKE US SOME SNACKS, AND LATER, LIQUOR.

ALL RIGHT. ONCE WE GET BACK TO THE SHOP...
NO, NO, NO!!
I WANT SNACKS NOW! I WANT DRINKS NOW!
じたじた
WHINE
FUSS
じたじた
FUSS
WHINE

EH? I'M SUPPOSED TO MAKE IT HERE?!

I HAD TO STOP BY HERE BEFORE COMING TO WORK EARLIER, TOO.

YOU KNOW THIS HOUSE LIKE IT'S YOUR OWN, RIGHT?

YOU'RE NO GOOD!
GRATCH
ARE YOU STILL DOING THAT WORN-OUT JOKE?
ALL RIGHT, FINE!
DÔMEKI, I'M USING YOUR KITCHEN!
RIGHT.

MOKONA'S GOING TOO! IT IS A PLACE MOKONA HAS TO GO!
DON'T YOU DARE EAT THE SNACKS!
BYOING

THIS SETTLES YOUR REQUEST OF ME, RIGHT?

YES.

MY READING OF THE SUTRAS WAS NOT ENOUGH.

NOT SO.
I THINK SHE WAS VERY HAPPY WITH THAT AS WELL.

...AND TO THE BEAUTIFUL DAY IN WHICH YOU LEFT...

...I PROPOSE A TOAST!

Continued

in *xxxHOLiC* Volume 10

About the Creators

CLAMP is a group of four women who have become the most popular manga artists in America—Satsuki Igarashi, Tsubaki Nekoi, Mokona, and Ageha Ohkawa. They started out as *doujinshi* (fan comics) creators, but their skill and craft brought them to the attention of publishers very quickly. Their first work from a major publisher was *RG Veda*, but their first mass success was with *Magic Knight Rayearth*. From there, they went on to write many series, including Cardcaptor Sakura and Chobits, two of the most popular manga in the United States. Like many Japanese manga artists, they prefer to avoid the spotlight, and little is known about them personally.

CLAMP is currently publishing three series in Japan: Tsubasa and xxxHOLiC with Kodansha and Gohou Drug with Kadokawa.

Translation Notes

For your edification and reading pleasure, here are notes to help you understand some of the cultural and story references from our translation of xxxHOLiC.

Page 4, Mokona's Fan

The character on Mokona's fan is that of longevity and congratulations, and the other accoutrements are reminiscent of the seven gods of good luck and New Year decorations.

Page 5, First Dream of the Year

On the night of New Year's Day (going into January 2nd), the dream one has is supposed to foretell the fortunes of the upcoming year. Particularly fortuitous things to dream about are Mount Fuji, a hawk, and an eggplant. That gives you an idea of why Himawari-chan says what she says about the eggplant later in the page.

Page 8, Madeleines

A madeleine is a cake-like cookie originated by the French. They consist of flour, butter, sugar, eggs and vanilla. It's said that the cookie was named by Louis XV after his former cook.

Page 9, I'll see you soon/ I look forward to it

What Himawari-chan and Watanuki exchanged in Japanese were the standard words said when one is leaving your home or other place one habitually inhabits (like a place of work or school): *Ittekimasu!* It's usually followed (or preceded) by the person who is staying behind saying *Itterashai!* In this case, it would seem a little odd for conversation in a school room in English, so I substituted some appropriate English dialogue.

Page 13, Two People Alone . . .

High school dramas tend to feature the popular, active-in-school-events character pairing up with the outcast. The popular character is very often a class representative, so a scene of two people alone in the class representatives' room at the beginning of a romance has become something of a cliché in Japanese dramas.

Page 55, -han/Osaka accent

The Osaka accent in Japanese is noted in several ways in Japanese. There are many vocabulary differences between the accent and standard Japanese, for example the honorific -san becoming -han. In general, the Osaka accent is thought of as a working-class accent, and is thus considered a little more earthy and more fun-loving than the more standard Tokyo accent. The translation tries to capture the spirit of the accent without attaching a regional English accent to it.

Page 64, Fox Spirit's Cart and *Oden*

Watanuki stopped to eat at a food cart being run by a fox spirit (*kitsune*) selling *oden* (skewered meat and veggies in a stew) in the final chapter of volume 3. There is more information on fox spirits and *oden* in the notes for volume 3.

Page 65, *Hyakki Yakô* and Being Saved

Watanuki and Dômeki were discovered as the only humans marching in a parade of spirits and magical creatures in the first story in volume 6, after which they were saved by the young fox spirit Watanuki met in volume 3. There is more information on the parade (the *Hyakki Yakô*) in the notes for volume 6.

A PLACE YOU CAN GET TO BY FLYING WITH A TENGU'S FAN!

Page 86, Tengu

Watanuki and Mokona first encounter Tengu in the form of Karasu Tengu in the first story found in volume 4, and more information on Tengu can be found in the notes at the back of that volume.

Page 88, *Dengaku*

Dengaku is one of Japan's oldest ways of cooking with miso. To make *dengaku*, one grills meat or vegetables on a skewer, then coats the food with a sweet miso sauce and grills it a second time.

Page 90, Cherry Blossoms

Cherry blossoms are a symbol of Japan. They are the most important sign of spring in the country.

Page 90, TV Programs

"True" stories of the supernatural done in documentary style have been popular on Japanese television for decades. They are usually cheaply made, but they can garner enormous ratings.

Page 137, *Shôgayu*

The name of the drink favored by Dômeki's grandfather is made up of the *kanji* for life, river, and hot water. A translation of the *kanji* would sound a little like "tea of the river of life."

Page 163, Ishidaya Saké

Made by the saké maker Kokuryu of Fukui, Ishidaya is a famous (and expensive) saké.

Page 164, Mahjong

Legend indicates that mahjong, the famous tile game, was invented by Confucius in 500 BC, but history first records it around 1880. By the first decade of the twentieth century it was no longer a game just for the aristocracy, and by the 1920s it was adopted worldwide (but most ardently in east Asia). It isn't in the scope of these notes to explain the rules, but here are a few particulars that will help you follow the manga. Everyone starts out with a number of points, and the points are transferred from the losers to the winners (through a very complicated set of rules). The first to draw a combination of three of a kind, four of a kind, or runs of three suited numbers (a single pair is also allowable in the hand, but all others are usually threes or fours) so that all fourteen tiles in a hand are accounted for, is the winner of the hand and is able to take points from one or more of the other players. Mahjong is used for gambling so the points also represent money. Most of the manga panels in this story show the characters winning using certain specially named hands (such as *Ten ho* or *Daisharin*) that receive large amounts of points. Mahjong, as played by Japanese rules, is a fast-paced game where players are constantly grabbing tiles as quickly as possible, so Kimihiro is at a very great disadvantage.

Page 166, *Xipai*

Yûko used the Chinese pronunciation for the word that means mixing up mahjong tiles.

Page 168, *Ten Ho*

Ten ho means that a winning hand is dealt to the player. Including three three-of-a-kind tiles and one pair, the hand is worth a great number of points.

Page 168, *Oya, Ko, Chi Ho*

Oya is the Japanese word for parent. *Ko* is the Japanese word for child. A *Chi ho* is the same as a *Ten ho*, but means a winning hand that is achieved after drawing only a single tile.

Page 169, Mahjong Manga

The rumors are true. There is a whole genre of manga anthology magazines that are devoted entirely to mahjong comics. Before you scoff at the idea of manga about a table game, you should take a look at the exciting layouts of tiles and melodramatic epic games in these manga. The three people "watching over" Yûko are Akagi, the title character of *Tohai Densetsu Akagi* (*Battle Tiles Legend Akagi*); similarly Tetsuya is the title character of *Shôbushi Densetsu Tetsuya*

(*Gambler Legend Tetsuya*); and Akina is the busty mahjong-playing beauty from comedy-filled *Super Zugan*.

Page 169, Mokona's References

These are three references that Japanese fans of mahjong would recognize. *Akûkan Zeppô* is a strategy for gambling formulated by master Michiru Ando. It advocates aggressive play when it seems that luck is not with you. *Seikyô* Mahjong is a gambling strategy found in the manga *Gin to Kin* (*Silver and Gold*) by Nobuyuki Fukumoto. And *Wareme-Pon* is a mahjong-themed TV show.

Page 169, *Daisharin*

This winning hand is seven pairs of one "suit" all in order. In other words, it's like drawing two straight flushes in poker that are exactly the same.

Page 169, *Chinitsu* with *Dora* 10

A *Chinitsu* is a winning hand where all of the tiles are of the same "suit." *Dora* are the bonus tiles, and Yûko has a bonus of 10.

Page 170, *Shôsûshi*

Also called the Little Four Joys, this winning hand includes multiple tiles of all of the four winds (North, South, East and West).

Page 170, *Nagashi Mangan*

A game that is won such that the winning player has never given away any tiles that help another player complete a three-tile run.

Page 175, Hiromi

The phrase, "The world of competition is a hard one, Hiromi!" is a famous phrase out of the perennial classic tennis manga, *Ace wo Nerai* (*Aim for the Ace*). Hiromi is the talented young main character.

AUG 2 0 2007

TOMARE!

[STOP!]

You're going the wrong way!

Manga is a completely different type of reading experience.

To start at the *beginning*, go to the *end*!

That's right! Authentic manga is read the traditional Japanese way—from right to left. Exactly the *opposite* of how American books are read. It's easy to follow: Just go to the other end of the book, and read each page—and each panel—from right side to left side, starting at the top right. Now you're experiencing manga as it was meant to be!